Grace Notes from a Bohemian in Wanderlust

poems by

Jeffrey James Ircink

Finishing Line Press
Georgetown, Kentucky

Grace Notes from a Bohemian in Wanderlust

For my father and mother—Jim and Dee, and Brother Jason, who realize that poetry is subjective, but like my poetry the best.

Publisher: Leah Huete de Maines
Editor: Christen Kincaid
Cover Art: "Winter Treeline," Cindy Lesky
Author Photo: Jeffrey James Ircink
Cover Design: Elizabeth Maines McCleavy

Order online: www.finishinglinepress.com
also available on amazon.com

Author inquiries and mail orders:
Finishing Line Press
PO Box 1626
Georgetown, Kentucky 40324
USA

Table of Contents

"Will-o'-the-Wisp"

I glimpsed a wispy milkweed seed
dancing on the air.
I grasped, came up empty-handed,
as though it wasn't there.
At last I finally caught it,
and cast a wish for me.
I pondered further (a second thought),
then cast a wish for thee.
I wished my love would hold me dear
and never leave my side.
Her wish—a better man, she said—
as she left on evening tide.
A gentle breeze appeared to blow,
and my wispy seed did stray.
Taken flight with other wisps
to offer wishes for other days.
Be wary of the wish you pluck
for there may come a day,
when what you wish for is mistook,
and the wish you want slips away.

"Elysian Fields"

The ensuing euphoria
was, quite simply,
the zenith of tranquility.
Like the grace notes scattered
throughout a musical composition,
or the masterful strokes of a painter's brush,
the intricacy in a flower's simplicity,
or an afternoon rain while the sun shines,
the company of another human—
whatever the state,
whatever your crème de la crème,
a veil of illumination fell over me,
my soul mired between two worlds.

All this, to the extent
I imagined myself in death's throes.
The final gasp, as it were—
a sublime episode of transcendence.
And for one lucid, epiphanal moment,
I glimpsed the dew-filled meadows
of Elysium, where I sauntered
amidst the lavendula and wheat tassels,
my face cooled by temperate winds.
Death, however, was not to be,
as fresh air coursed through my bosom.
Among the living am I,
seared with visions of Shangri-La,
if you will—
unattainable for the present,
and with a hint of lavender
left to tickle my nose.

"When the Queen Bee Dies"

[The following events were recorded by my brother, a self-taught apiarist, and subsequently translated into poetic form by me, while observing our hives in Central Wisconsin during early Fall of 2020. These findings have since been shared with The American Bee Journal, the American BeeKeeping Federation, The Bee Conservancy, and Scientific America, among other notable institutions and periodicals, in the hopes of advancing our knowledge of bee culture and preserving their existence as vital creatures in our ecosystem and—ultimately, for humankind's survival.]

Cloaked in a veil of secrecy
beyond the scope
of human understanding,
the world of the bees'
readies for a solemn fête
for the queen has taken her last breath.

Word spreads quickly
throughout the hive
and the buzzing swells—
blaring trumpets stifled
to a faint decibel
of a mournful sort—
to the brink
of uninterrupted pandemonium.

In the matriarchal tradition
unique to the social order of bees,
preparations and flourishes
are underway to lay the queen to rest.
A continual whir of drone wings
keeps her body cool,
while oils—collected from native flora—
are applied as a rite of cleansing.
Wrapped in willow leaves and rose petals,
the queen is whisked away
on the shoulders of her subjects—
no words are said, no memorials read,
for that is not the way of the bees.

Not entirely bereft of emotion,
with pomp and circumstance
befitting her regalness,

a somber processional swarms forth
to honor her legacy,
under guise of hallowed dirges,
privy only to the colony.
Even the flowers bow in reverence,
spilling dew drop tears
onto the meadow soil
as they share in a collective melancholia.
Enclosed in a beeswax sarcophagus
filled with royal jelly,
and adorned with willow catkin,
the queen is placed on the back
of a dragonfly where—
under a canopy of dusk
and worker bee escorts—
she is swept away
in a quiet splendor
to lands of milk and honey
and otherworldly places.

In every way that Nature
has fed my soul,
none more poignant
have I seen in this.
Oh! what pity is found
in the places we do not know.
Tell the beekeeper!
Long live the Queen!

"To the Poet"

I am seldom bereft.
Of ideas, that is.
Serendipity shines
upon my brow.
                  To wit...
in an excerpt from a dream,
I stared at the devil who,
after making a little old lady
consume herself until
she became nonexistent,
experienced death by a sneeze,
while bird gods drank from the
land of milk and honey
and juncos flitted under the guise
of a silver slipper of the moon,
for which I gave odes to.
                  This is why I stare.
I reap, sort and spew forth
all notions racing through my mind
to avert a state of satiation.
I am an anomaly of what you think you are—
an amalgamation of what you are not.
I am a recycler of second thoughts
to no end but to fashion my own—
truthful notions that cannot be debated,
denied or disputed.
Plausible if not altogether infallible
and most certainly dictatorial.

                  A proper fetishist self-driven
                  into becoming a harbinger
                  for posterity's ears,
                  at the behest of a universe
                  that is not conscious
                  of my existence.

For in poetry,
no greater truths
can be found.

"Butterfly Wings"

Adrift and sauntering…
that which finds respite
in my company
for a fleeting moment,
unencumbered by agendas.
Yet our collective logic
makes us none the wiser.
Perhaps we are undeserving
of flights of fancy?

"Tell Me Again About the Lilacs"

Teetering precociously
on a tightrope stretched
between birth and death,
we journeyed along the high wire
in a formulaic dance
of balance & free will
to a future we had not a clue.
Vowing each to the other
until the end of our days,
hearts embraced amongst
the lilac blooms in the home we kept.

As the last grains sift through the hourglass,
here we sit with patchwork thoughts in tow.
A now sedentary existence parcels out
stolen moments with which
to squint between the shutters
of our 24 foot by 30 foot space,
each wondering who the other is.

I am told we were once full in love but I forget.

For in our youth,
we know everything—
except what it is like to become aged,
when no one cares
what we knew in our youth.

The passing years push us forward,
while we inexplicably take steps in reverse.
The infant becomes the child;
the child the adult;
the adult…the infant once more.
A contented life worthy
of the proverbial eulogy,
yet deafened by empathy.

How did it come to this—
this shunning by silence?

Tell me again about the lilacs…

"Bird gods"

The aerodynamics of a bird
are an engineering feat.
I have yet to see a human
flap his arms
a thousand feet in the air,
swoop down,
and land without a stumble
on my bird feeder.

"Bello"

We, in tow,
with vestiges of yesterday,
etched upon the visages of today.
Weathered and bruised;
a topographical map for the ages.
Brilliantined kaleidoscopic swatches
covering our personage
no matter the narrative's bent,
like a watermark of our
trials and tribulations.
We, who are spectators of our own specters,
unable to shed the skin of our former self—
the times of our lives—
enshroud ourselves in remnants of a false face.
The question lies not with the mask
but what is hidden beneath it.

"Half-Past 3 a.m."

Whenever I rouse from a dead slumber,
half past 3 reads the clock's number.
A game of hide and seek I deem quite cruel,
as I am the one to be played for the fool.

It's my subconscious, I think, behind this trick,
seems the magic hour I know not when to pick.
When the lights are out and I count my sheep,
extraordinary things happen once I lay me down to sleep.

> *With brandished longswords and a yew-carved bow,*
> *Templars and Robyn vow silence to all they know.*
> *Peppery cowpokes do-si-do beside yellow Mountain sage,*
> *bathed with sprinkles of pixie dust that glitter the desert stage.*

> *As a frigate pitches and heaves on North Atlantic ocean swells,*
> *barnyard animals on Christmas Eve chant verses from "Carol of the Bells",*
> *Brown-haired genies in cashmere kaftans steal home for a snooze in their bottles*
> *and look…off the neighbor's roof zooms Santa's sleigh at full throttle!*

> *Durin's kinsfolk in solemn procession with mithril and gold in tow,*
> *St. Peter's indulgence begged by souls fleeing the bardo.*
> *Dewy saunters through green leas in Tipperary,*
> *reveals a humble wish granted by a charmed Celtic faerie.*

> *A cosmic spaceship shoots the Milky Way with a child at the control,*
> *Apache and Cherokee rain dance 'round the ceremonial totem pole.*
> *Steampunk locomotives whisk day-trippers to everywhere but here,*
> *while circus clowns with painted frowns reassure us there is nothing to fear.*

> *Peaceful evenings lying 'neath a sky so wide,*
> *amidst white pines stretching into the star-filled eventide.*

These unabashed sentiments flow freely from my tongue,
youth truly need not be wasted on the young.
Doffing my street clothes to retire for night,
I ask for wisdom and forethought to do what is right
in my prayers I recite before I doze,
as this dogged day draws to a close.
I reach for the clock set to wake at 6, you see,
and I pause, give thought, then reset it for 3.

"Land of Milk & Honey"

There is a place.
And in this place
there is no noise.
No clapping hands,
or waters lapping,
or children laughing.
The timbre in your
mother's voice
is silent.
No birds peeping
or winds blowing
in this place where
noise is void.
No crickets chirping.
No clocks ticking.
No thunder crashing.
or guitar picks picking.
There is no need
for whistles or bells.
No reason to hear
the shrieks and yells,
or the lamentations of the
scourged and oppressed.
A lack of noise
precludes the need for
screeching tires,
or sirens squelching
raging fires.
Or bibless babes who sob
from the confines of cribs.
No coughing or sniveling,
or belching or driveling.
And no war wages,
defying the sages.

For there is a thin buffer
between image and sound
in your mind and therein
lies this place of quietness,
a tranquility found.
Pursuit of an idyllic frontier

is nothing quite so novel.
Best sought beyond the boundaries
of one's humble hovel.
Many have doggedly
searched in vain
with aspirations yet unattained.
A place of refuge
for rich and poor,
for weary wretches left forlorn.
A reckoning forged
by gadabouts and ordinary louts,
by poets and kings,
of odysseys that inspired
choruses to sing,
in their quest for solace
and eternal esteem,
to chase what has been,
thus far, an impossible dream.
Standing fast while
nations crumbled,
left unfulfilled, deeply humbled.
And in this vapid place
there are no words.
And with no words,
there are no sounds.
And with no sounds,
there is infinite quiet.
An altered state.
An alternative plane.

The necessity to wait
is fruitless,
for you are already present.
The promised land—
Elysium, Camelot,
Arcadia and Shangri-la,
Kubla Khan's Xanadu,
Utopia, et al.
And in that place
a wellspring reveals
with death comes the wisdom

sought throughout the ages
and the keys to the kingdom
will be given you.
All this too shall come to pass.

"I Saw the Silver Slipper of the Moon"

I saw the silver slipper of the moon
and the silver slipper of the moon saw me.
Floating in the cloudless heavens above,
still and vigilant for humanity to see.

"You are well, I trust?" said I to the Moon.
"Hello! Indeed!" was the Moon's reply.
His demeanor was quite jovial and gay,
with an inconspicuous twinkle in his eye.

Trepidation aside, I wistfully professed,
"Lovely night for a stroll, Mr. Moon, don't you think?"
"It certainly is; your way is most luminous,"
replied the Moon with a smirk and a wink.

"I wish you for my own," I emphatically declared,
*"a souvenir, of sorts, with no others to share.
Safe and sound in my pocket I would keep thee,
no offering could quite compare."*

"Alas, I must deny such indulgence," said the Moon,
*"for my presence here is by otherworldly design.
Imagine! How would others make their way,
without the Moon's light to shine?"*

But the Moon's counsel I heeded not,
and I impetuously swallowed him whole.
Moonbeams shot from my eyes, ears and nose,
a quite unsettling sight to behold.

Never was seen a blacker evening,
without the Moon to shine o'er all.
Folks bumping into each other for lack of light;
the Earth reeling from my cosmic faux pas.

The errors of my way I was versed,
and I coughed up the Moon in haste.
To covet such an object…for shame,
when such objects should remain chaste.

I begged the Moon's forgiveness
(for the Moon's a formidable host).
"You won't be the last, I fear," he laughed.
"The Moon for yourself? Quite a tale to boast!"

So I gave the Moon a nod,
and bid goodbye as he set sail.
"Always reach for the stars, my boy", he beguiled.
The worst that can happen is you fail."

"Strangers"

I once told a complete stranger
she had the most beautiful eyes
I had ever seen.
She was a brunette.
People say I'm only
attracted to blondes,
but this one was a brunette.
She said thank you
and we parted ways.
I bumped into this brunette
several months later
and I reminded her I was
the brash guy who told her
she had the most beautiful eyes
I had ever seen.
She smiled and asked me,
"Who are you?".
I said, *"Does it matter?"*
"It does to me," she said.
****

I still tell that brunette
how beautiful her eyes are.
She smiles and asks,
"Who are you?"
I remind her that I'm her husband
and we've been married
for thirty-five years.
She says, *"I don't remember."*
I tell her I love her
and she says, *"Does it matter?"*
I tell her, *"It does to me."*

"Lemmings Are People Too" (or "Bleus Musings")

She sat at the
next table over.
A cup of tea
and half-eaten croissant
with cream cheese
set beside her.
Hazel eyes now shuttered
to conceal her calm slumber.
You would never know
she was dead.
Her face bore the slight smile
of someone privy
to something I was not.
The lemmings prattle on about
how they know everything.
Maybe they're already dead
and simply don't know it.

"I Stared Down the Devil"

I stared down the Devil
and the Devil stared down me.
A game of wits for the ages,
some would say,
played 'neath a red bud tree.

Not one solitary blink
'tween the two,
eyes intently fixed.
Time will tell who is true,
and who is up to his tricks.

The prince of the dark arts—
quite unawares—
unleashed a powerful sneeze.
For in his zeal to fetch my soul,
he poo-pooed his shrub allergies.

So sayeth Demosthenes,
'nothing's easier than self-deceit',
be ye politician, solicitor,
or a trader on Wall Street.

With a blink and a howl,
the Devil shrieked, *'Unfair!'*
another go at it, he'd druther.
I smiled and said his chance was spent—
his presence is heavy, and he ain't my brother.

"This coup—there but for the grace
of the Prince of Peace go I,
by my side His staff and rod.
Your foul expulsion was a sign from above—
they call it an Act of God."

With tail between his legs,
the Devil absconded with a smirk.
Oh! To be a shadow
in his valley of death,
and watch him go berserk.

So if Old Scratch pays a visit
with ledger in hand,
make sure you go Dutch treat.
To the victor go the spoils
wherever the twain shall meet.

"Ode to the Moon"

(Aunt Ruthie nicknamed my brother "Moon" upon his birth as his head resembled the shape of this heavenly body.)

"A wise man's question contains half the answer."—Solomon Ibn Gabirol

How do I release a fish into the water to ensure its survival?
To which my brother responded, *"Here, I will show you."*
How do I distinguish one tree from another in the forest?
To which my brother responded, *"Here, I will show you."*
How do I become a steward of the land?
To which my brother responded, *"Here, I will show you."*
All this and more I have learned from him.
All this and more we have shared.

The years pass and our days are not idly spent.
I ask and he answers—until we can no longer "do",
at which time we pass the days paging through scrapbooks,
reveling in our trifles and eccentricities.
On one occasion well into these—the thick of our elder years—
I ask my brother, *"How does one die?"*
He pauses, then answers, *"Here, I will show you."*

And I follow him deep into the woods on a wintry evening
while a fading Sun clings to the tree line.
Trudging through ice-covered snow, we arrive at a stand of sugar maples.
"You cannot kill a tree by merely taking its sap," my brother reflects.
He kicks and scrapes up a handful of dirt and puts his nose to it.
"The earth is good here."
Contented—he sits, leaning against the tree.
"It will be bitter cold this evening," he avows.
Looking deep into my eyes, he says, *"This is how you die."*

The rest is silence.

By this time the Moon has replaced the Sun on the treetops
and her light leads my way as I retreat to the cabin.
I am alone but for the heavy quiet which fills the space.
I stare at the fire's ephemeral flames
which flicker and leap with a final gasp,
embers of a life fully lived.

And for a time I struggle to recall
one thing my brother had taught me.

My eyes catch a spider near where the wall meets the floor,
painstakingly spinning its web. I leave it be.

…and I remember now. My brother taught me well.

I rise and open the door—the wind has picked up,
the temperature has plummeted—
just as my brother said it would.

And the Moon has reached its zenith.

"All the Good Martyrs are Dead"

Amongst us walks a being
under no cloak of secrecy.
We are privy to him, her, or they,
(as it is not gender exclusive)
mindful of its presence.
Wreaking in self-exposure,
the Martyr...
back hunched,
shoulders heaved,
arms dragging—
a body burdened by the
weighted conscience of
perhaps tens of hundreds.
With a captive audience,
(willing or otherwise)
the Martyr espouses a tale of blame,
a mixture of truth and deception,
fraught with the provisional
"woe is me" through line.
An allegorical tapestry
contrived and woven so smartly
the Devil himself would find
pity upon him.
Once complete,
this masochistic ritual assuredly gains
the trust of the unwitting,
for this Martyr warys not
of self-righteousness.
The Martyr revels in the reluctance
of its ill-fated, half-hearted,
and under-appreciated deeds.
Oh, the humanity!

The sheer tonnage
of selflessness is mind-boggling;
a psychological torture
that carries with it a load
quite unbearable for most.
Wait for it—wait...
can you hear the applause
from the stander-by's

who rise for this *fête*?
Take a bow,
dear Sir or Madam or whatever
you call yourself,
in hopeless reverence
of your accomplishments.
Be advised, however,
the gratitude which you seek
ebbs and flows,
as empathy is in short supply.
The show has come full circle,
none but for the silence;
the Martyr needs a respite
before its next diversion.
Au revoir! Mea culpa!
But alas, regarding my
particular situation,
I can lend neither ear
nor credence to your pleas,
for, 'tis the pity…
all the good martyrs are dead.

"Good Friday. 2018."

I sat in a swale of patchy woods,
where my father sat before.
His terse, dry wit filled my head,
as my feet tapped the forest floor.
The wind was quiet,
but for the brushes' flutter,
and as softly as Dad's voice,
I heard the wind mutter.
"Be still and know
that I am here."
I faced the wind and smiled
and spoke without fear.
"That Bible verse
is the word of God,
be wary, Mr. Wind,
of where you trod."
The next sound I heard
had a timbre so true—
that of my father,
a voice I most certainly knew.
"Don't you worry," Dad chagrined,
"I know of what I speak.
This is one occasion, my son,
you may choose to be meek.
Though your concern for credit is admirable;
I hear your call for submission."
'Be still, my son,' again he spoke,
'I've got the author's permission.' "
With that, the wind turned silent,
this Friday had been good indeed.
The day I was touched by my
Father's wisdom
amongst the box elder trees.

"Travelers"

[I see travelers on a journey...]

In the midst of a moment
when death's door
is but an arm's length away,
there—prostrate,
lies a spent life.
Minutes measured in hours,
seconds in minutes,
wallowing in a hive of thoughts—
fear, anguish, relief, trepidation,
of what was,
might have been,
and is to come.
Alone—a fraternity of orphans—
searching for a profound revelation,
a longing for resolve.
While the chapeaus vary,
ours is a universal tale.

*[...where we are all poets
of our own mortality.]*

"Excerpts From A Hollywood Dream"
(North Hollywood, 1999)

THE SCENE:

Lost Angels.
Mother Earth's ant hill of humanity.
Shaken, burnt and drowned
in a perennial festival to cull the herd.
The cheapest facelift in town
and no one bats an eyelid.
Unlike most mothers,
Lost Angels is void of empathy & heart,
chewing her beggars like cud,
then apathetically spitting them
onto the pavement.
What remains is cloaked in a red carpet
of broken pipe dreams.
Not everyone plays,
but everyone gets a participation medal.

THE BEGGAR:

I venture West to add to the carbon footprints
of those who've come before me—
the tsunami of Beggars
on borrowed time,
bent on beating the odds,
gleaning to grab a crumb
and stake a claim in the bastion
of wrap parties.
How inane.

THE BLONDE:

Waify, petite surfer girl,
bored with the California Dream
and looking for someone to do.
A Plain Jane—though her name was Grace.
A pleasant diversion—
my door was curtain number 3.

I fell into Grace before falling out of her.

Who said the apple doesn't
fall far from the tree?

THE NOBODYS:

Smelling like cleaned, dirty laundry
with taco stains & Tabasco sauce
for added measure,
two White boys & a Mexican from the
shitty side of NoHo appear.
I forgot the third dude's name—
something with a "Ch" or an "ez".
Black Leather Jackets without the black & leather.
As common as the Beggars and Blondes
who flock to Lost Angels—
happy-go-lucky and looking for thrills,
they stumble onto the scene
because their pants are drooping
past their asses.
I smiled.

They say at least one spring songbird
signals a red herring day.
I saw hundreds of them that morning…
I just didn't hear the right one.

CUT TO:

The mood swing changes as abruptly as
the Santa Anna winds.
The Nobodys circle the Beggar
while the Blonde lurks in the wings
twirling her hair and waiting for her
next ingénue.
Phoneys with attitudes.
And the dance climaxes.

As I jostle and writhe in bed,
the culminating events are a vague haze.

I could humor you
and share what I remember.
But my friends have never known
me to be a masochist.

"Good luck at being famous, Dude!"
And with the screeching of tires and laughter,
the Nobodys and their Blonde whore vanish.
All that remains are a few orange peels.
Not a portent of death.
Much worse.

EPILOGUE:

Parts well-played, no script in hand,
the Beggar, the Blonde, and the Nobodys flee the stage.
The ghost light is lit.
The sense of ego is palpable in Lost Angels—
as are the scents of want that
waft up from Ventura Boulevard
into The Valley,
across Mulholland,
fingering down Laurel Canyon to
Sunset and the PCH.
Both taint.
And neither is more prevalent than the other.
I am engulfed by all that one could desire,
but lacking in everything one needs.

To all the bitches in Bel Air,
all the children you love to hate in Culver City,
all the Nobodys and Blondes and sulking Beggars—
my sundries are packed,
in search of greener pastures.
It's a red delicious day
for I return to the tree,
where maples drip syrup and
honey pours from combs.
"Carpe diem"—"let the Beggars beware".

By the way, you can go home—
and all the Lost Angels can go to Hell.

"The Juncos Keep Coming"
(for Bob)

I strewn seed on the ground for the birds.
It must be junco food because that's all I seem to attract.
I don't recall reading that on the bag— *"Junco Seed."*
I watch for a time—
little birds and little beaks pecking
at the ground in a feeding frenzy.
One junco works itself into such a state that it crashes
into the window I'm peering out
but manages to fly away unscathed.
I'm told that if a bird gets stunned
and falls to the ground,
you're to grab it immediately
and warm it until it revives or it may die.
So says Iakona.
I never question Iakona
when it comes to our feathered friends.

It's odd to think of Death when watching birds feed.
(Unless one crashes into your window
and you don't grab it and warm it.)
But I do.
So many souls in such a short span of time.
So many that I have grown weary of it.
Death.
When answering its cue,
like the passing of the sun and moon,
the parade of Death comes swiftly
and discriminates against no one.
The Danse Macabers turn and wave goodbye
to the living while their procession passes.
What pleasantries!
As if to say, *"See you later!"*
I can hardly wait.

And the world keeps spinning.
And the paraders keep marching.
And people I know keep dying.
And the juncos keep coming.
I don't want to have to revive any.

"The Chimes at Glen Mar"

The chimes in the yard once filled with glee
when winds would blow, I'd turn and see
the chimes, by chance, dance out their notes,
enchanting tunes that none had wrote.

With flashes of glimpses that ebb and flow
and me—with memories firmly in tow,
a lilt, that timbre, all too sublime,
it needn't matter there was no rhyme.

Now their tenor is a mournful sort,
no happy tunes that come to court—
wary, they are, of those in keeping
with he who is present while sleeping.

Dirges sound of one who walked
these paths quite often and seldom talked,
but left a footprint even so
his kin to follow, that they would know
this place endures, a shimmering star,
for 'tis his namesake—they call Glen Mar.

"Finches"

*(dedicated to the memory of my friend
and theater mentor, Robert Geuder)*

A glint of yellow swoops and flits
about the treetops,
merrily warbling in a familiar,
whimsical dialect,
bringing me solace
as well as pause for reflection,
and it occurs to me…
at the very moment
I am shuttered for eternity,
I wish to glimpse a goldfinch
from my bedroom window,
as the finch never disappoints
in pleasing my senses;
how joyous—to greet Death with a smile
and a chirrup.

"Continuities, Part 2"

7:31 a.m.
Late October

I sip coffee and stare out the window.
The Russian sage is dead;
its husks flutter but
the wind is still.
Peculiar.
I look down to see a chipmunk
jostling the sage stems
while attempting to eat
a Chinese lantern.
A squirrel pilfers the bird feeder,
spilling seeds onto the head
of a solitary nuthatch
pecking at the ground;
it doesn't seem to mind.
I glance back and notice a spider
dropping from the wood beam ceiling
on a single silk strand.
I leave it be because my brother
would be disappointed if I killed it.
The crusader pennants flutter in the breeze
and then it suddenly begins to snow.

I wonder what happened with
that chipmunk and the Chinese lantern?

"Variations on a Nature Theme"
(or "The Peepers' Concerto No. 30")

On cue, the setting sun
unhurriedly trades places
with a slipper moon,
as a red haze lifts to reveal
a Northwoods pastiche.
The air is laden with the nutty,
turpentiny sweat of earthen-fed,
water entrenched timber.
Flowering birch catkins
dance in the wind,
while the dwarf willows curtsy,
dressing the stage
for this evening's recital.
The pike and the perch
swim a jig in the murky shallows,
and a mayfly ballet
matriculates in the air overhead.
Grouse drumrolls reverberate
across still waters as the forest gathers
like a conflagration—
tealing teals,
eagling eagles,
and blue heron's heron'ing—
all jostle for balcony seats
during the prelude to the peepers' concerto.
To regale such a
spectacle to an industrialist…alas.
Bravo! Encore!
A miraculous thing to behold—
me in the front row
of Nature's amphitheater.
I expect even the harshest critics
will be left with mouths agape.

"Death Is No Flower"
For Marsha…

The lilies placed
where 'neath you lay,
a token, a solemnity,
for words I cannot say.
If Death were a flower,
these would suffice,
like the peal of wedding bells
and the toss of rice.
If Death were a flower,
I'd pluck thee from the ground,
so as not to grace the sanctity
of a burial mound.
Yet salvia and iris flourish
and die of one accord,
as do daisies and sage
that straddle the towpath board.
April sprouts make
the death prattle moot,
as Death on Earth is final—
there is no substitute.
For a flower is not death,
its petals to be reborn;
yet a soul bereft of body
departs this world, whence it is torn.

www.ingramcontent.com/pod-product-compliance
Lightning Source LLC
Chambersburg PA
CBHW020225090426
42734CB00008B/1215